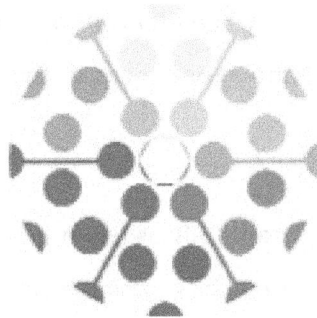

THE RIPPLE EFFECT GAME

for Personal and Planetary
Transformation

1st Launch Edition

Cindy M. White

www.RippleEffectGame.com

PERMISSIONS

For reasons of confidentiality, names, circumstances, and other identifying information of people mentioned in this book has either been left out or changed. In all cases, the stories faithfully reflect the ideas, attitudes, and experiences of the people in the stories mentioned.

ACKNOWLEDGMENTS

Thank you to Deborah S. Nelson, who faithfully assisted me in the publication process. Deborah is a constant demonstration of what's possible when you work inspired. Thank you to David V. White, my amazing Dad for editing this book. Editing thanks also goes to Dawn Joy Marks and Doug Scott. My deepest appreciation goes out to all of my many teachers, personally known and not, from workshops, courses, and hundreds of books, all of which this book humbly follows. My most influential mentors have been: Dr. James Spira, PhD, my massage teacher; A true healer, meditation mentor and friend, the late Dr. Tim Tupper; Paramahansa Yogananda and his Holy Lineage; Eckhardt Tolle; Li Hongzi, founder of the Falun Dafa form of Chi Gong; My parents David and Darlene; my twin brother Steve; my great friends; and a kitty named Lacey. Last but not least, thank you to all the miracle workers who play, for you lift the game to new heights with your great stories and talent.

EDITIONS

This is the 1st Launch Edition of The Ripple Effect Game for Personal and Planetary Transformation. As this game continues, new favorite stories will emerge. These may be included future editions. You can always print out the latest version of the eBook, or buy the newest version of this book from www.RippleEffectGame.com, or though Amazon.com. Please get extra copies to send out, spreading the "ripple effect"!

This book is lovingly dedicated to
the entire world.

May we take the path
offered within
and do what we came here to do;

SHIFT THE PLANET

Table Of Contents

PART 1 — THE JOURNEY

Chapter 1 — Preparation

Chapter 2 — The Blessings

Chapter 3 — The Power of Focus

Chapter 4 — Living In The Miracle

Chapter 5 — Managing Your Game

Chapter 6 — Blessed

PART 2 — MY JOURNAL

PART 3 — MY STORIES

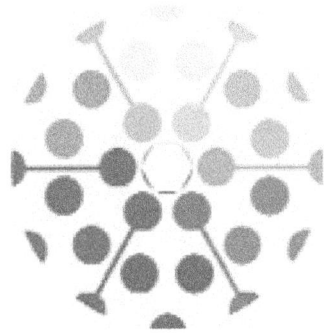

THE

RIPPLE EFFECT

GAME

PART 1 — THE JOURNEY

THE RIPPLE EFFECT GAME
For Personal And Planetary Transformation

Definition: A Ripple Effect. Concentric waves or vibrations which emanate outward and inward infinitely, caused by one simple action, such as a pebble cast into a pool of water. A domino effect. The cumulative effect of this domino effect.

Introduction

Sometimes we go through life, and no matter how hard we try, the outcome is not what we expect. We ask ourselves, "Why do I keep falling into the same patterns?" What does it take to create a better, more satisfying life?" When we're down, depressed, unsure, or feeling hopeless, we need a way to jump-start ourselves to get back on the happiness road again to a positive, loving, and more abundant life.

Like a magnet, we pull situations and people in, based on where we're focused and how we feel. So, once our vibration changes, so does our whole life. This is the key! There are many ways to heal our wounds, understand our past, and become motivated. But ...

Have you ever played a game to consciously generate positive energy wherever you go for an entire month, to create a miracle in your own life and in those around you? This is what we accomplish by playing The Ripple Effect Game. This book will guide you for the next 30 days to take actions that lead to wonderful moments, deep insights, and a newfound joy. What happens becomes nothing short of life changing.

Congratulations! You have just embarked on a journey like no other, joining the many who create transformation by playing The Ripple Effect Game.

This book is the complete Play-At-Home version of the game. It's written in three parts: "The Journey" inspirational narrative and workbook questions to fill out, "My 30-day Journal", and "My Stories", to summarize your deepest insights, most remarkable blessings, and favorite stories that come out of playing.

Get ready to have one fantastic miraculous month after another! There is no way to lose in this game. So sweet are the precious moments if the game is shared with another, or with a group. You will meet new people, create your own unique journey, and all the while know yourself to be a powerful, loving presence in the world. This in turn brings about personal and planetary transformation while having a lot of fun.

In a paragraph, here's how to play:
As you read through the book, complete the workbook questions. You can also begin journaling right away, writing your entries any way you wish. Each morning, you pick a daily Theme that balances or supports you throughout the day. Then choose a few blessings to enact from the list in Chapter 3. Life will present opportunities for you to fulfill these blessings. You'll also look for the spontaneous blessings that happen without any effort on your part. Next, log those notable experiences as they happen, both the "good" and "bad" ones. Share your stories, and away you go!

If you like the bells and whistles of a video game and social interfacing on the world wide web, try the game's official web site at: www.RippleEffectGame.com. Sign on for a world of transformational fun! If you would rather have a book in your hands and meet in person to share the journey, then the Play-At-Home version is for you. You can play either or both ways.

Within the next 30 days your life will be on the super highway of the miraculous! You'll have fantastic stories to tell. Generating positive energy by offering blessings or bringing love to a situation creates a magnetic condition for good to flourish. It facilitates ease and clarity. It heals everyone involved. Offering something positive to the world is like using a key which opens doors to love, community and new situations. It helps us feel and know that there's a buoyant, undefinable essence governing our life. Playing this game, we are an integral part of a grand experiment to better the world.

As you play the Ripple Effect Game, opportunities present themselves which were formerly unnoticed. Creativity abounds. Really good things happen, one after another. There is a difference between how most humans live, and how a miracle worker lives.

Typically, most people tend to be focused in these areas:

- "What's wrong?" (focusing on the negative)
- "What needs to get done?" (living from our "To Do" list), and
- "How can I entertain myself?" (self-indulgence)

All of these focuses are perfectly normal, even responsible ways of thinking. But the problem is, they don't generate the results of positivity, creativity, or deeper satisfaction we truly want. For example, "What's wrong?" is the worst thing you can ask of any situation. "What needs to get done?" tends to make us robotic, living life from our heads not our hearts. And we all know that seeking joy and entertainment in a selfish way isn't the path of greatest joy.

It is by finding a way to give to another, or to declare what's GREAT about right now, that appreciation sets in. Why reach for the carrot that never arrives? This game is founded on the magic that results when focusing on the following types of questions:

- "Where's the next blessing? Where's that magical moment?"
- "What sweet little thing can I do for someone else?"
- "I'm in a breakdown. Now what are the insights in this?"

Staying in these focuses brings a whole new type of experience to us. We find that it even propels us toward the happy, rich and fulfilling life we want. Rather than being a ping pong bouncing from experience to experience, randomly joyful then suddenly upset, the blessings we engage in day in and day out create a more solid environment for us. Then, opportunities abound.

Staying in the question, "What's a creative little way I can bring joy to the situation in order for everyone to be uplifted?" you are living a formula for success. When we ask, "What are the insights within the problems of our life?" we can make every experience a mini-miracle.

With blessings as your goal, the types of encounters you have will become synergistic. You'll meet people you wouldn't ordinarily meet. You'll attract ones who are also radiating this positive frequency. Your life will be enriched. Meanwhile, it's quite easy and fun! The Ripple Effect Game is a tool which can help you in unlimited ways.

We also accomplish a miracle by acknowledging our breakdowns. These are always viewed as positive in this game, for they literally are the catalyst for our new awareness—the stuff from which our break*throughs* are made. When you realize that you can glean 10 or more different insights from one bummer in your life, you connect the dots in every experience, as a master does.

Your "bad" encounters can be a complete celebration, seen as an unopened gift designed perfectly for you to launch towards an incredible breakthrough. And the new insights you receive will remain with you forever. All the while, this simple formula keeps life an ongoing pleasant experience, as it's meant to be. In short, it changes everything.

Because of these new focuses, life can easily take on a whole new meaning and purpose. Before long, you are living an effortlessly potent life actively and consciously generating as many blessings as you can, and logging as many discoveries as you can. You will know what it means to say, "Everything serves my highest good".

Unlike other games, there is no way to lose The Ripple Effect Game. Just make an agreement with yourself to stick it out for at least 30 days. You don't need to change, and you don't need to get ready. Wherever you are in life is the perfect place to begin a ripple effect of good for yourself and others. Life, exactly as it is, becomes the perfect canvas for you to create personal and planetary transformation.

The good vibes you will feel from playing are fun and contagious. It comes alive as you share this adventure with those you care about. And the more people playing the Ripple Effect Game, the more positive energy is generated for the planet. One miracle at a time, you are a part of transforming it all.

Me? A miracle worker?

Don't worry, it's not as hard as it sounds. You can DO IT! Don't think of this as a skill you don't have. Everyone offers blessings all the time. Now, you're merely noticing them and keeping track. You get to decide at all times how often you play, and how passionately or casually you want to play this game. You take the driver's seat for creating your own miracle month.

You will receive benefit from the slightest action or insight. You don't need to seek out ways to generate positivity; they will present themselves to you naturally. All of a sudden, you'll be a part of an obvious situation where there's an opportunity to provide a blessing, and you'll know at the time what's needed.

Sometimes you'll scratch your head in pause just after some situation and say, "Wow. That was just a blessing!" It happened without any input or effort; without a word. You were just there and noticed it. That's how miracles unfold, as natural as the sun comes up. So journal about it as your "Spontaneous Blessing" for the day.

Then, let's say something else happens that didn't go too well. It was an accident, an offense, a missed appointment, an argument. This becomes material for an insight! After writing the problem down, let it go. Then get curious about it. Self-reflect. *Want* to learn something about it. And you'll find a silver lining appear out of what happened every time. As soon as you ask for the insight, these negative situations become the set-up for your wonderful new perspective. Even if you realize, "I never want to do that again!" congratulations—you gained an insight, closed a door on something, and now have more clarity in your life.

We just don't realize the incredible value of our issues. In this game, problems of any kind are positive. They are championed because not only do they lead to an insight, they are the fuel for our spiritual growth. They are the kindling we need to transmute ourselves towards our highest good. So we come to LOVE our breakdowns. (Really?) Really. We see our issues like knots in a rope we climb up, in order to enjoy the horizon from the vantage point of our new breakthroughs.

But personal breakthroughs are just the beginning. One kind gesture on your part could be literally life-altering for another. Plus, it's fascinating to experience that a small act of kindness can pop you out of a bad mood. Unhappiness is usually the result of too much concern for yourself. Whereas, playing The Ripple Effect Game is all about making someone else happy. This just causes joy for both of you!

What you will do this month could be just the dose of love someone badly needs. Kindness to others always touches you both immeasurably. We may never know the impact of some ripples we generate. Some, we'll never forget our entire lives. Do you recall this email story that circulated around?:

> There was a high school boy who was completely depressed. Each day was treacherous for him. Finally, he planned to take his life. He cleaned out his locker and made his way home, a suicide note already prepared to place on his pillow that evening.
>
> His father was a grumpy and critical businessman, gruff and overly work-oriented. He'd never taken much time out for his son. That same day, something special happened.
>
> At work, the Dad was given a lapel pin by an employee which read, "YOU MATTER." This random act of kindness gave that man such a pause, his heart swung wide open. No one had ever offered this kind of gesture to him before. He reflected about how he'd never told his son this, and so in turn resolved to give the pin to him that night.
>
> Heartfelt and touched by the random act of love, the Dad eagerly awaited his turn to honor his son in this same way. A slumped and defeated son arrived home. His Dad sat him down and told him all the ways he was proud of him. He shared how valuable he was, named a few examples of how he recognized the boy's strengths, and proclaimed how lucky he was to be his father. He then presented his son the pin.
>
> Incredulous, tears streamed down the boy's face. Then he melted in his father's love. The boy pulled out his suicide note, ready to leave on his bed. He told his father that he didn't need to kill himself anymore. He didn't feel the need to resort to that dire a solution any longer. They embraced as if for the very first time.

We don't know just how special the love we give to another is. But we can trust that it is. Loving acts are received in ways that help people for their own highest good. It frees up issues of the past and restores relationships. You will see that playing The Ripple Effect Game can be this profound for you.

There is no one way to play The Ripple Effect Game. Any experience that you consider "a blessing" is one. Just keep reading this book, journaling, setting your morning theme, bringing someone love, and watch the miracles trickle forth. You'll be inspired each passing day. When hitting a breakdown, quickly ask for an insight.

There is no limit to how much good can be generated. Every game, just like every person, is completely unique and uniquely valuable. When players always benefit, all the players transform. You'll come to witness a new structure has emerged—one of a connected, loving Human Family who's there, and who really cares. It's always been there. But now, you can see it.

There is no other spiritual game out there exactly like this, where transformation is the prize and your own life is the treasure map. You'll witness the wonderful bonding that occurs when one shares their "aha" moment after struggling in a breakdown, as everyone leans in to hear it, bearing tears of joy.

I acknowledge you for stepping onto this path, choosing to believe it is no accident you are here. For the whisper of the Infinite always calls to us. And the Realm of the Miraculous is ever with us, inviting us to express our Soul's true Nature, which is Love.

Thank you in advance for all the blessings you'll send out. May you enjoy many miraculous moments with countless sweet blessings coming in return. May this repeating tendency be your way of life, and a new norm for your every waking day.

Chapter 1 — Preparation

Clarifying The Process

Clarify for yourself your primary goals for playing. Do you want to be happier? Do you want spiritual growth? A better connection with others? Are you bored? Stressed out? Merely curious? All of these are great reasons to play this transformational game. Clarifying your own desire to play will help you to benefit even more.

Write down all of your **intentions for playing** in the space below. Include as many reasons as you can. If you need more room, use the space on the previous page.

_____

_____

_____

_____.

You can use this game and this month to make progress in these areas. Let the Ripple Effect Game be your compass as you navigate through life for a while. Give yourself the gift of playing all out, with a curious open heart, and see what happens.

Begin each day by scanning the Themes on page 26, and picking one that calls to you. Or, you can make up your own theme. The right one will be obvious, because it will be your medicine, restoring balance in you, or supporting your day ahead. For example, "be patient all day long" or "be spontaneous all day long". The theme is your "tone" for the day. When no blessings are happening, you are experiencing life through this lens. Vary these to suit you.

Once you have picked a Theme, next choose a few blessings from those listed on pages 27-31. Let life present opportunities to bring these blessings about. Some blessings require several steps. Some will be more challenging than others. As you naturally move through your day, watch out for that appropriate moment, then enact the blessing.

Shortly after, write about it on your cell phone, or computer, or in your journal. It's easier to record blessings right after they happen. The sooner you jot down your experience, the more likely it is to remember the details of it. Write about it colorfully, yet briefly. Perhaps you'll mention what it did for others, or how it was for you emotionally, capturing the "miracle-ness" of it.

Regardless of the intention, if what happened was negative in any way, then list it as a breakdown. Reflect on the situation, then transmute it into a positive by finding some insight about what happened. You may never think you'll find even one, but they come. Insights may take time to present themselves. That's perfectly OK.

In the narrative section of your journal, feel free to vent about what went wrong. This can start softening your bummer. Eventually you'll gain more understanding, and then even more. Stay curious about the hidden lesson for *you* rather than writing too much about "them". As you do this exercise, you'll see how this part of the game can be surprisingly rewarding.

The journal in the second section of this book is for 30 days. Try to write a little every night. Write the date at the top of each page and your Theme for the day. Then, list the "Blessing" highlights that occurred. Intend for a few each day. Always list any breakdown. Find at least 5 insights around it. Try to convey what happened in about 30 words (or 2 lines).

In the "narrative" part, write whatever you want. This is your private space to record in. You can write about your inner feelings. You can recount the day in greater detail. You can vent, or draw pictures, or doodle. You can write your secret longings, or fears, or greatest hopes. It's private, and it's all yours.

Just be aware not to dwell in projection and victimhood. Projection is seeing your own issues "out there" in someone else but not in yourself. The annoying truth is:

It's always our own stuff, or we wouldn't have been triggered by it. Vent, but then unlock the lesson; find an insight in it.

As you write about your day, you may realize there were more blessings you hadn't noticed. How many times do good things happen, and we don't give it a moment of our time? The nice part of using the journal is it will contain your whole miracle month with everything all in one place. If you like to write a lot, it is recommended to go get a blank, lined journal. Some people use a spread sheet on their computer.

At the end of just one month, you will have experienced so much. You'll get to reread your prized journey-into-greatness with fondness and joy.

Your First Day Of Play

A good way to begin is to let the Theme of your first day of playing The Ripple Effect Game be: "observing and information gathering", and let the blessings you enact be for yourself!

All day long, notice how things show up in life, merely as they are. Just witness what's happening. Watch yourself. Notice what you call a blessing, a miracle moment, and what you think is a bummer. Just observe. At that time, or at the end of the day, journal it all in a matter-of-fact sort of way. "This happened, that happened, etc ..." Leave space after entries in case you want to say more.

After each blessing, notice the specific "ripple effect" in your body from the positive event that happened. Notice exactly how it feels when negative things happen. Write about this.

Now, guided by your deeper wisdom, contemplate the "bummers" that happened. See if you can come to any insight about them. Sometimes it takes a night's sleep. Sometimes it will be immediate. Try to brainstorm at least 5 positives from each negative experience. If you're up for the challenge, go for 5 more! Finally, feel the ripple effects after having found the insights. Write the physical and emotional sensations you experience.

Journaling

You'll record all the work you do in your journal. Once you realize you experienced a blessing or an insight, write it down as soon as possible. Aha moments come and then leave our minds sometimes if not jotted down. Don't lose those pearls by telling yourself you'll remember them later on. Even if you put down just five words, it's best to log as you go. This is important, so "wow" moments aren't forgotten.

At the end of the month, miracle stories will bloom. You will appreciate the ability to reread them later on in life. As much as possible, document the blessings, deeds, situations, emotions, and all your insights. It could prove very helpful to pick a time each day to write, and stick to this same time.

This is also the place to journal your frustrations and complaints. Really give yourself permission to rant and rave! It is far better to vent privately in a journal than to gossip to all your friends. Or even worse, to bottle up your emotions never releasing them at all. Having vented and released disappointment tends to change the story, letting the steam out of it. Journaling usually reveals a silver lining when complete.

I begin journaling in this way: At first, I don't know why, but I'm irritated. Then, a barrage of wicked remarks comes out, which feels great because I know that no one will ever read my vicious verbal tornado. Getting it out gets me off of it. From somewhere, that still small wise voice emerges and speaks to me. From somewhere, I am comforted. I arrive at a new perspective.

Journaling evokes our own wise counselor, one that doesn't cost $125 per hour. The process of journaling prevents us from dumping unexpectedly on the people around us, which isn't so nice.

Tracking your blessings does a number of good things for you. For one, it gives you that extra self pat on the back. It lengthens the time you spend acknowledging the positives coming into your life. How many times do we receive something wonderful, or find something lost, or just have a great day and never take even a second to be happy about it? Journaling brings things into perspective. It charts the actual path you are taking to emerge as the beautiful being you are. Highlighting our blessings attracts more in.

Week at a Glance

This game can be played entirely and magnificently solo. Or you can play along with a partner. And, it's really fun to play in a group. You can call each other to share how your experience is going. You can collect support, divulge struggles, offer an ear, and hear some really cool stories.

You may wish to set up, or join a weekly Play-At-Home game. Much can be learned by listening to what's going on in another's journey. There could be a tendency to forget to play for a few days. Your group will be there for you, and visa versa, keeping each other on track throughout the month. The groups who have played all report they've bonded with their fellow "ripplers", some saying that physically coming together was the best part.

The following is a suggested basic formula for breaking down the game; the readings, exercises, and journaling into 4 weekly increments:

Week 1:   During Class: Scan the whole book, fill in ALL workbook areas, share "Intentions for Playing" add new Themes and Blessings. Home Work: Begin journaling, pick a Theme every morning, read Intro., Ch 1, Ch 2.

Week 2:   During Class: Share your week, share more workbook entries, talk about the previous reading. Home Work: Read Ch 3, Ch 4, journal.

Week 3:   During Class: Share breakdowns, find 10 Insights from 1, write them down, talk about prev. reading. Home Work: Read Ch 5, Ch. 6, journal.

Week 4:   During Class: Share insights, Review your month, talk about the previous reading. Home Work: Finish the book if you haven't already, write a miracle story, review highlights, put at the end of the book.

Final Day: Pick a date, either on week 4 or shortly after, and throw a Ripple Effect Game Party! You could have a pot luck, or meet at a restaurant, however you like to celebrate. This is where you share your favorite story; your Miracle Story. And you acknowledge the "Best Player" and their accomplishments.

Other ideas? Invite family and friends to this last day to hear your stories, and to inspire them into playing the next go around. The healing never stops when you play The Ripple Effect Game. Let it be an ever expanding process of contagious fun and fulfillment.

The Game for teens, and the Golden Years

Young people love to play games! Invite your Teens to the challenge. This game has no guns, no violence, and no war. It's also a multi-faceted learning tool. The benefits at any age are numerous. But can you imagine teens:

- Developing the skills of creativity, self-reflection, kindness, and giving
- Growing in self-esteem through positive actions and positive strokes
- Playing a game that involves physical activity in the real world
- Learning a formula for how to turn breakdowns into breakthroughs
- Enhancing their writing skills
- Mastering what it means to be a "miracle worker" in the world

Now imagine the impact on seniors if they could experience these benefits:

- A revived sense of purpose
- Mental stimulation
- Enhanced creativity
- Connection to others
- Acknowledgment for all of their contributions
- A greater sense of aliveness
- Getting to play and have fun!

All can benefit from playing The Ripple Effect Game. The more players there are, the more interesting stories we get to read, and the more miraculous results will be produced!

Terms and Conditions

However you choose to set up your game, there's one major rule: please make a commitment to finish the 30 days. Don't quit! Keep on playing, even if you've got a lot on your plate, even if it seems like things aren't going too well. During this game, issues have a way of surfacing. But, they also have a way of unwinding themselves in the most desirable of ways. If you stop playing for a few days, not to worry. It's perfect. Just get back in the game again.

Initial if you'll agree to the following:

1) I will bring my creativity, my talents, my integrity, and my depth; in other words, my best self to The Ripple Effect Game. _____
2) I will play with a curious mind and an open heart. I will be tolerant and gentle on myself, and on everyone else. _____
3) For continuity and for the benefit of everyone, once I begin the game, I will commit to it for the whole 30 days. _____

This gift is yours. Enjoy all it has in store for you. May it be like no other!

Ready Set Go!

You've just made a personal commitment to yourself. Choose a convenient date to begin, and write your start date here:

_____.

Count 30 days from this date, and write your completion date here:

_____.

Pick what time of the day you prefer to log your daily blessings and to journal:

_____.

If applicable, what day or evening is best to come together weekly?:

_____.

Put these dates on your calendar or day planner. Try your best to keep these appointments with yourself. Afterall, this is for you, not anyone else's benefit. At week 3, you can write "One week left" to help excel you down the home stretch. Congratulations! You've just embarked upon a very promising adventure.

Chapter 2 — The Blessings

Themes And Blessings

Every day you'll create a Theme, like "Being peaceful all day long" or "Being a good listener all day long." This Theme stays with you all day. It is your guiding mode you return to, no matter what comes about. In a sense, a governing Theme is a type of blessing you exude all day long. Pick a theme that balances you or supports you. This is a very powerful part of the game. Each morning decide on a theme, and log it in your journal. There is no steadfast rule on which to choose. Just play around with this. You could actually do nothing else. Different themes cause different types of interactions.

Blessings are specific happenings or action steps. On the following pages are some examples of blessings you can extend. Try any of the following that feel good to you, and add some of your own in the spaces provided. (Inventing new blessings gives you points in "Invention" online.) Some blessings you'll want to give over and over. Some will feel scary. Don't shy away from these! Within any difficulty is surely an opportunity to push through your own blocks. And this is what you want. Take on experiences to stretch yourself, and look forward to the breakthroughs that follow.

I recommend beginning by taking baby steps. Maybe you'll want your theme to be "Be gentle with yourself all day long" and set no goals with how many blessings you'll enact. When you get your bearings, then give blessings, acknowledgements, etc... Remember, there's no wrong way to play. Everything you do (or don't do) can be done with Love. Every step leads to greater insight.

Themes

Be an observer of the blessings that already are, all day long
Stay in gratitude all day long
Be peaceful all day long
Be a giver all day long
Be a listener all day long
Be Love all day long
Be agreeable all day long
Don't say much all day long
Observe all day long
Be creative all day long
Be a good friend all day long
Be like a child all day long
Be joyful all day long
Be guilt-free all day long
Be honest all day long
Be humble all day long
Be lazy all day long
Feel open and expansive all day long
Experience bliss all day long
Be meditative all day long
Make amends all day long
Be a good friend all day long
Be alone all day long
Be relaxed all day long
Be patient all day long
Be thoughtful all day long
Be spontaneous all day long

Now invent your own themes:

_____

_____

_____

_____

_____

_____.

Every day offers you a potential for new blessings. These are the positive spontaneous actions or interactions which make you feel good. They are also intended to
make others feel good. They are specific tangible experiences. Even if it's a sweet
thought about someone, you can quantify this as a "Blessing". When you feel a
blessing just occurred, it did. Write it down.

Self-Blessings

Begin the game by giving to yourself first! Here are some ideas of self-blessings:

Take a long bath
Get a new haircut
Get a manicure and/or pedicure
Get a massage
Spend time on hobbies
Write in your journal
Go exercise
Meditate
Bake / Cook
Go shopping
Clean out a closet
Give yourself something you've really wanted
Travel somewhere
Learn something new
Sign up for an Adult Ed. Class
Spend a whole day in nature

Spend a whole day in sweet silence and solitude
Spend most of the day in bed
Watch a great movie
Nurture yourself in your favorite way
Give away/donate something you don't need
Read
Paint
Fly a kite
Belly laugh
Sing
Play a musical instrument
Look at your photo albums

Invent some of your own self-blessings:

_____

_____

_____

_____

_____

_____

_____.

You can add your new blessings onto the website. You'll gain "invention" points. Make sure yours hasn't already been listed.

Blessings For The World

Now from a full cup, give these out to the world:

Send a thank you card to someone
Leave a really nice message for someone
Post something really positive on Facebook
Smile at someone
Hum a happy tune in public
Thank someone you normally don't thank
Talk to a stranger
Make a new friend
Pretend you're on vacation in your own town
Tell someone you love them
Make steps towards resolving differences
Be receptive when someone tries to give to you
Forgive someone completely
Do what you've procrastinated doing
Have that heart-to-heart talk with someone
Spend quality time loving a pet
Take a dog for a long walk, yours or someone else's
Look someone in the eyes with more presence
Apologize when appropriate to do so
Listen to someone a little longer
Be a leader
Hold your tongue when thinking of saying something negative
Give someone the right of way, with pleasure
Pray for someone, whole heartedly
Throw a party
Make someone laugh
Lend someone a hand
Go play frisbee, or tennis, or paddle ball
Gift a beggar $1-$20
Go play with your children / grandchildren
Play with someone else's children
Make a special meal for someone
Create a poem for someone, and share it

Make up a song
Sing in the shower
Ask someone for their advice
Give someone something of yours
Be generous in some way
Volunteer at a favorite organization
Thank someone for something they did for you in the past
Make a funny face until someone laughs
Tell a joke
Look deeply into someone's eyes with pure love in your heart
Hold someone's hand
Give someone a really nice hug
The next thing that upsets you—let it go completely
Share what lesson you've just learned with someone
Share what lesson you're still working on
Tell someone your big dreams in a way that they get that it'll come true
Praise someone
Shower someone with love
Give someone a brief massage
Ask someone for some specific support in your life
Tell people three things about yourself, in conversation
Reveal a secret you've been keeping
Let something petty go
Finish a project you've started that was put on "park"
Resolve to quit something you need to stop doing
Pick up some litter
Tell someone that you think the world of them

Now invent your own blessings for the world:

_____

_____

_____

_____

_____

_____

_____

_____

_____

_____

_____.

Try adding these onto the website, too. As you share your creativity, you'll bring more to everyone's game.

The Slightest Blessing

A blessing may not always be tangible. It can be a thought that once you have, brings you gratitude. It can be taking better care of yourself. It can be your own good mood. Happy, fulfilled people generate a positive force field around them, which can be felt. This affects many. Your presence, however silent, spreads out into the infinity of all.

A blessing can be listening to your inner voice, and following your gut. It can be what you didn't say, that saved a cascade of drama. It can be choosing to forgive, even if you aren't speaking with that person. A blessing can be refusing to wear those tight shoes anymore.

Because of the nature of ripple effects, one effort can reap untold benefits. Think of rock stars like the Beatles. Were they working hard or just doing what they loved? Songs, quotes, a planted tree, a donated bench, the over the top special day you give to a child; these are simple things you can do that live on to benefit a millionfold throughout the ages. That is how significant you are. That is how powerful playing The Ripple Effect Game can be.

Many on earth have become heroes in our eyes, because of their deeply loving ways. Jesus Christ is the perfect example. He taught the Golden Rule, "Do unto others as you would have others do unto you." Matthew 7:12. Dr. Martin Luther King Jr. is a great example of a man so impassioned, he crusaded an entire country to stand for equality of all men. His speech, "I have a dream..." lives on in our hearts. Surely included among our heroes of Love is Mother Theresa, who said, "There are no great acts, just small acts with great love."

These heroes were being themselves while surrendering fully to a Higher Cause. Playing the Ripple Effect does this for you too—it helps you surrender to your own Higher Cause, while unlocking the keys to your personal growth. If you simply play along and don't quit, within one month you will walk triumphantly as the living master and miracle worker that is the essence of who you truly are.

Make room for the possibility that mastery is no different than sharing your own true essence out into the world. If you asked any hero if they felt what they did was hard, they'd possibly say, "All I remember is it was entirely worth it."

This book asks only that you step into mastery in your own unique way. It may be hard to imagine ever making the difference heroes have made on the planet, but just know that you already are a hero. You've already accomplished so much.

Scan your life and recall your triumphs, your many achievements, and all the things you do well. There is no one in the whole world like you. Don't ever forget how special you are! The world knows this and needs you. The world is complete because of you.

Chapter 3 — The Power of Focus

Damaging Focuses

Do you realize that there are a lot of things vying for our attention, and that most of it is negative and superficial? We watch TV, we play video games, we buy stuff, we worry about our weight, we dread Mondays. We eat poorly, we are bothered by the people around us, we suffer from lack of funds, and on and on and on. This mental matter is hectic and chaotic. It fills up our minds so that there's little room for clear and productive thinking.

These concerns swirl around our head in a repetitive pattern keeping us returning to the same old problems, and revisiting the same bad feelings. Offensive in nature, this activates our ego, and we react with negativity to the negativity. All the while, damaging focuses gobble up our precious time, and separate us from our omnipresent good. Maintaining a damaging focus erodes our very lives, as it drowns out all perspective on the magnificence that life is.

Further, paying attention to the negative and the horribly offensive has a debilitating health impact on our heart. According to the Centers for Disease Control and Prevention, the leading cause of death in America in 2007 was Heart Disease, with an annual mortality of over 600,000 people. Cancer came in a close second with more than 500,000 deaths, and Stroke was third at a little over 100,000.

Again, in 2009, Heart Disease was the #1 leading cause of death, Cancer was second, and chronic lower respiratory diseases came in third. These statistics show that we are a population in which our hearts are assaulted. It would follow that the most important life preserving action we could take to better our health is that of restoring, healing, and providing the most optimum environment we can for our hearts.

Another report from the Centers for Disease Control found that 65% of all deaths had one common element: Stress. Coping improperly with stress leads to many other diseases such as depression, alcoholism, prescription and non-prescription drug addiction, and nutritional maladies due to a poor diet.

And let's be clear: Stress is mostly self-inflicted by improper choices, and therefore is largely avoidable. It is entirely possible to minimize the stress in our life. We can do this by redirecting our focus from a negative mental one to a positive, heart-centered one. And this is what the Ripple Effect Game is all about! It's time to bring the focus back to what is life enhancing, to what is Loving.

Currently, we have to deal with the national debt, terrorism, war, violence, both on the streets and on the silver screen, poverty, stress, foreclosures, and catastrophes from climate change not to mention our own personal survival issues. Violence and fear is sold as exciting entertainment. Most video games implant horrible scenarios into the impressionable minds of our children. No wonder we feel stressed out! It would seem that there are more negatives in life than positives. But this isn't true.

Unless we actively implement a new focus, such as what this book presents, we are by default adopting any troubling focus driven by the media, our parents, and who knows. We hold the erroneous assumption that if it's on the news, we must be informed about it. But we don't realize, it is designed not only to inform us, but keep us panicked, mired in the terror, and glued to it's nightmare. Does it deserve that much of our worthy attention?

Ask yourself these important questions:

- "Does watching random acts of violence on TV make any actual difference to the condition of those problems?"
- "Would disturbing images right before going to bed be good for my sleep?"
- "How much negativity do I think I can take, without it having an impact on my health?" and
- "What percentage of horror is beneficial to my life?"

True, not all mainstream information coming through our media channels is negative. The point is to actively discern where we place our focus each moment, and not unconsciously take in whatever is in front of us.

How many times do we listen to stories, watch things, and stay in situations which don't make us happy? How many times is our focus on what's wrong? Why must we rubber-neck when driving by a car crash? Our focus is off track. It needs to be brought back from the awful, to the awe-inspiring. What is required is to be aware and to keep choosing positive, meaningful things to focus on. It sounds pretty easy, but it's a skill that needs practice.

People spend a lot of time focused on what they don't want: bills, gossip, the latest scandal. Our subconscious mind doesn't hear the word "not" or "please don't give me..." It just faithfully brings us more of exactly what we focus on. So, if you don't want debt, or stress, or ill health, simply stop thinking about them forever more. Instead, continuously think about financial abundance, relaxation, and a healthy body. Once there, get excited about all the ways you will experience being rich, being easy going, and having vibrant health.

You can attract many ways to achieve what you do want, just as you've attracted ways to perpetuate what you don't want. When living in the results of your favorite dream becomes a habit pattern, when positive expectancy is your dominant emotion, it will manifest.

But, we brood for hours over what's wrong with us. An off-handed remark can stay with us for a lifetime. We think that staying focused on what's wrong is staying on track. But we are only dwelling in negativity, and by doing so, we are ensuring that more of it will be heaped upon us. No wonder we are weary.

Shifting as quickly as possible to the positive as soon as we catch ourselves in the negative opens space for a full acknowledgment and celebration of each and every moment as it is. Wouldn't you rather have a life of gratitude, seeing the cup half full, and living in that sense of fullness virtually all of the time?

The time has come to live, move, breathe, and experience life from our hearts! The power lies in our focus. Our focus creates our destiny in life. It governs our mood. It then becomes a magnet for more. So, consciously redirecting our focus away from what we don't want to what we *do* want, makes for our most positive, meaningful, and potent life.

The way we do this is by claiming our freedom of choice, then redirecting our attention away from where it causes us stress, to where it brings us upliftment, peace, and joy. Focus is like the rudder that steers our course, catching the positive winds of Love, as we sail sweetly onwards to our most cherished destiny.

Examine Your Reactions

Emotions are often the outcomes of how we interpret the situations we find ourselves in. **Briefly, write a situation that made you feel scared, frustrated, wronged, or sad;** specifically something you are having trouble letting go of. Then, under each situation, **write your typical negative reaction. Third, write a new interpretation, one that helps you see it in a better way.** To do this, imagine hearing someone else's view. Imagine an explanation that brings you out of outrage and into compassionate understanding. Example:

Situation: Someone wreaklessly speeds down the freeway, and cuts you off almost hitting you.
Old interpretation: Shock, outrage, then a nasty judgment. "What an asshole!"
New interpretation: That man could be taking his pregnant wife to the hospital, speeding to get her there on time. Or, "I remember racing cars when I was young. I drove way faster than that!"

Now it's your turn. If you need more space, use your journal in PART 2 of this book.

Situation:

_____

_____

Old Interpretation:

_____

_____

New Interpretation:

_____

_____

Situation:

_____

_____

Old Interpretation:

_____

_____

New Interpretation:

_____

_____.

Take another inventory: Notice how much better you feel imagining your new, more positive interpretations, whether they were even true or not. Do we actually know exactly what's going on with other people? So why torture ourselves with a bad mood that comes from a low interpretation? Wasn't it nice to imagine more innocent or even positive reasons for the injustices that happen to us? Think of all emotions as food. Try to keep a healthy emotional diet for the next 30 days. See for yourself if it makes a difference.

Negativity usually depletes us. It can create reactive behaviors, like acting out in retaliation, which only feeds further harm to the world and makes no one feel better. Positive interpretations, either imagined, or gained by gathering more information about the matter, have an energy balancing effect. They tend to help us think more clearly. Positive interpretations elevate moods and give us a light buoyant feeling.

Remember: Regardless of how harmed or victimized you may be, the interpretation of what went on is always a choice. And this choice is alway ours. Our choices can lead to greater compassion for our fellow man as well as an overall peace and flow in life. Not reacting poorly maintains our calm abiding peace, even if we don't get our needs met. We think we're justified when righteously angry. I say nothing else matters when we're pleasantly on track with our peace of mind.

Allowing the world to dictate our focus is just silly. We have many times the products, toys, food, and gadgets we used to have just 30 years ago. Yet, we are less peaceful, and less healthy. Products have become more readily available, but have they given us more deep or lasting happiness? It begs the question, "What really is the picture of a qualitatively better life?"

There are always going to be a vast number of choices bombarding us. This is why commercials, magazine ads, the news, and media coverage are so prevalent. It works. It broadcasts non-stop what we're supposed to buy, or believe in, having everything to do with making millions in profits if you "buy into them." But it ends up having little to do with what is truly best for you. Therefore, ads and news need to be heavily scrutinized.

Driving the point home, we live in a time when prescription drugs are sold as the primary method for regaining health. Natural remedies are not allowed to claim they heal or will treat conditions. Senior citizens are so over-medicated they are the largest group of drug addicts in our medical system. Those who resort to self medicating via recreational drugs are thrown in jail for years. In many ways, our modern world is very off kilter. To think otherwise is to be naive. It's probably wise to assume we are all brainwashed to a degree, and we must de-brainwash ourselves.

Yes, we have some heavy problems. But as long as we are numb to the repercussions of these epidemics, they will continue to pollute us, terrify us, grab our precious attention, and cost us dearly. We need help with our daily lifestyle, at every turn.

There's one great wake-up call you can give yourself to make your life work—It's by redirecting your focus to the positive, the helpful, and the Loving. Shall we let the world's latest drama steal our attention, time and time again? Or shall we claim back our lives by using the power of our focus?

Remember this: Our life thrives where our focus lies. So we focus on blessings, on community, on creativity, and on self-awareness. These focuses walk you through a different doorway. They return the miracle back to your moment.

As we shift our awareness around thinking, buying, noticing, contributing, and how we become happy, we make vast amounts of room for our deeper desires to emerge. With the time we save avoiding drama and a toxic lifestyle—terrorism for news, violence for excitement, medicating for health, and consumerism for filling up—we move forward to creating our own set of goals and focuses for a life of true fulfillment. Life becomes gentle. We become alive. Our ship sails where *we* want it to go.

Powerful Focus

There is a commodity we all have, and don't realize its wealth. It is our focus. Our attention is like a hose watering the garden. It supports everything in its field to grow and flourish. In this aspect, it is unconditional. This is the trick about focus. We have become focused on what we don't like, and what we don't want, never realizing that by our very focus, we call in the horror, the poverty, and the fear. Unknowingly, we're watering the negativity on the planet.

Our turning point is when we regain control, sitting in the driver's seat of our power to decide where we'll place our focus. When we harness this ability, and bring a lot of positive energy to it, we begin to master this power. We can manifest. We get it, realizing that all we're ever doing is bringing forth results with the power of focus.

Hopefully this is good news, that we bear the burden of responsibility to become the masters of our own destiny. It is our own unique path we tread, a path that is known from within, not copied from another. Leaders aren't mired in what's wrong. They access from a greater place. You too have your own internal fortitude. Leaders don't turn back and live in the past. You too can you stay focused on this brand new, ever alive moment.

When you do this, you will:

- quiet the noise
- remove the stress
- make the right choices
- allow your whole body to function more healthily, and you
- make room for your creativity and pure possibility to abound.

Correct focus does all this and more. Focus is like fertilizer to the garden of your every dream.

Write several areas of your life you wish to flourish. These become your **goals for playing:**

_____

_____

_____

_____

_____

_____

_____.

Fantastic!! And So It Is.

Chapter 4 — Living In The Miracle

Healing

Whatever we do, there is always a ripple effect. This impact occurs simultaneously in ourself, and out into the world. When our task is to be a miracle worker, there is a domino effect of ever-spreading good flowing inward and outward. Blessings affect your total health; your cells, your mood, your biochemistry, your thoughts, your dreams, and your very life force. This game, if played continuously, ends up generating a healing in you.

Of the many benefits, you may experience greater health, happiness, community connection, appreciation, and self-love. You may have better self-understanding, better relationships, and a feeling of being empowered. There may be a lightness and ease about you, a deeper connection with Source, and an inner peace that comes from your kind and giving way of being.

It's esteem building and a glorious satisfaction to experience your days becoming brighter and your activities infused with sweetness. You'll know yourself as a miracle worker on the planet before long. So will others! Once again, you have always been one. This is a just a great opportunity to reveal your own diamond within.

The Soul's Voice And The Ego's Voice

Listen to your Inner Voice. It will lead you to what to do, what to say, and where to go. Your still, small voice aligns you with the flow of life. Just listen and trust, listen and trust. You are always guided by your Soul's voice. We have angels and guides who also assist us. Try calling upon this help often throughout the game. It is said that help will pour forth. Here is an example of how to call in Divine assistance:

"Father / Mother God, Holy Spirit, guides, and angels present.
I call forth your Divine protection, guidance, support, and love.
Thank you so much for all your great assistance with _____.
In loving gratitude, I say, "So be it! And so it is. AMEN."

The more you call on help from Divine Sources, the more you bring yourself into alignment with the ever present Higher Good. Help is always available but must be asked for.

We have another voice we know all too well, that of the ego. It shouts at us, usually in the tone of a scolding parent's cruel message. It makes us blatantly aware of our wrongdoing. Don Miguel Ruiz, in *The Four Agreements,* calls this voice the "Mitote", or thousand screaming voices. This is the domesticated mind, passed down from our down-trodden ancestors. It wants to survive, any way it can. While the ego has a positive goal of keeping us alive and safe, it's means are not always healthy. Today, we don't need all the animalistic mechanisms geared toward self-preservation. Our ego needs to be tempered by our own voice of love, forgiveness, and compassion.

We all know of the image of a little angel on one shoulder, and a little devil on the other. At any given time, we can heed the guidance from either of these aspects. Which voice we listen to will determine whether we take the high road or the low one.

The little devil's voice is the ego's voice. It serves us by being our master of survival. However, driven merely by fear, manipulation, control, attachment, lust, greed, selfishness, and an overall warped view of reality, the ego is a horribly misguided mentor.

Most people, even if they've read the Bible, or hundreds of spiritual or self-help books, continue to listen to their ego. Why is this? Because it speaks first, and speaks the loudest. Secondly, it is because somewhere along the line, we believed what it says about us; that we're unworthy. So, hooked in, we allow this nasty critic the main stage. Whenever you hear the voice of cruelty, immediately interrupt it with the following message. Say this emphatically to yourself:

"You are such a good person! What a nice person you are. You are really thoughtful. You're awesome."

You can make a vow right now never to allow negative self-talk anymore. When it comes up, immediately replace it with the above, or a personalized statement that's meaningful to you, and speak it aloud. Self-praise reverses the needless damage we give to ourselves, and brings us back to reality.

Additionally, make a mental note to contemplate and find an insight around this dynamic. Collect the reward for figuring out what's underneath such a charge that led you to scold yourself. Get curious, more than offended, when this happens. Your breakthrough is right before you.

As we sharpen our ability to recognize the difference between our Soul's voice and our ego's voice, we gain access to our Soul's voice. It is always calm, wise, and compassionate. It is honest, but doesn't force Its wisdom upon us. It comes from a greater depth of reality, so has the bigger picture in mind. It is connected with the highest outcome of all involved. It must be called forth. It is the voice of Love.

The ego will feel mean, rushed, worried, and self-interested. Never in the present, it is focused on the future or the past, which can create worry and regret. It feeds on resentment, and hopes for retaliation. Illusory in nature, it produces insecurity and separation. It pipes in without notice. Repetitive in nature, it punishes relentlessly and unjustly that same error, endless times. It is the voice of Fear.

Everyone knows about these two voices. You can see people who are tormented by debilitating beliefs they carry around, undermining their every goal, hurting themselves their whole lives. This one revelation can give you compassion for others. People hurt. They feel separate. They try so hard but it's a struggle to live their life. And this is why they act out in ways that don't serve anyone.

Some people have it really rough, and are worn thin. This one recognition—that others are in pain—can transform our short lifetime by giving us the compassion needed to be a comfort zone along the tumultuous path of life. Cultivating our ability to stop being at the mercy of the ego's voice is a great habit to learn. It will enhance our confidence as well as demonstrate to the world how to stay peaceful amidst life's ups and downs. As we gain these abilities, we naturally bring peace to those who suffer.

Accessing Inner Guidance

Here's an exercise for helping you find the answers that are most beneficial for you in making your best decisions. First, drink a glass of water, to be hydrated. Then, stand straight and tall. Ask to fall forward or backwards marking a "yes" signal. Then, ask yourself to fall in the opposite direction for a "no" signal. Relax. Don't try. Just ask, and wait for the feeling that you are being helped to fall a certain way. It sounds funny, but it works!

Now test this by saying, "My name is _____" (say your name). Wait and allow. You should feel yourself falling in one direction, designating your "yes direction." Next say, "My name is _____" (pick any other name). Wait and allow. You should feel yourself falling in the opposite direction, for the "no answer."

When I do this, I feel my body quivering. Then, sure enough, it falls in the direction of the correct answer. It's pretty incredible. **Practice this now.**

We are much like a tuning fork. When we ask within and get a "yes" on a question, this "yes" is literally the echoed Yes of Truth within the Universal Known. We are merely bringing this information to us through our body. This is called "muscle testing".

Another way to access our Inner Voice is just to tune in keenly to our body and listen. A "yes" can feel like a wave of excitement. When something is right for us, there is a lightness and an openness, a sweet warmth, or a softening of our muscles. In contrast, if we ask within and an answer is "no," our body registers this as discord all throughout. The heart quickens, adrenalin pumps. We may feel a headache, a weird rush of blood, a contraction, or a heavy, sinking feeling.

This is how lie detectors work; by registering the body's constrictions and relaxations. There are many minimal body cues to notice. However it is for you, begin to notice.

Our amazing body contains a vast amount of wisdom. It is contained on the cellular level, and within the subconscious and unconscious mind. Much information can be accessed. Always ask for permission to do this for another.

When asking questions, be open to what your body's wisdom says vs. having a strong bias one way or another. Most of our beliefs are adopted from others. The value of accessing our innate knowing helps to clarify our deepest truth. It helps us make the best choices for our highest good.

Once you've learned this skill, you can get all sorts of information such as determining what vitamins or supplements you need, or what food you're allergic to. You can see if a new career choice is right for you. You can inquire about a love interest. You can ask any "yes" or "no" question. **Practice this technique now.**

If you aren't getting clear signals, ask your questions more specifically, or in a different way. After getting answers, follow this guidance! Trust your greatest teacher—your own Inner Guidance.

Getting Guidance from the World

The entire world can be a mirror for the answers you seek to know. Here's how:

In the beginning of the day, ask your question. Write it down in your journal. Then, throughout the day and week, stay receptive for any messages to come in from wherever. It could be words on the radio, a billboard, the TV, or overhearing someone's conversation. When an answer comes, you'll know it.

Example: You ask, "How can I heal my aching back?" You take your car in for an oil change, and the mechanic tells you, "In addition to needing oil, your car is out of alignment."

Bingo! The word, "alignment" reminds you to call for a chiropractic adjustment. This is how messages come to us, for our highest good.

There is one more method of accessing guidance, through the dream state. Here is how:

At the end of the night, write your question or concern and hold it in the forefront of your mind right before falling asleep. Ask for a deep restful sleep and a clear answer to come forth upon waking. Leave the journal and pen close by. When just waking, recall the question and listen. Drift back into the half asleep half waking state. Ask again. Give thanks. You will receive your answer right away, or soonafter.

The Pearl In The Negative

Normally, we don't spend time self-reflecting on all our problems and issues with appreciation. Therefore, we often miss the pearl of insight each negative occurrence offers. Oh, we notice and realize for a brief moment that we screwed up. We see in hindsight what we could have done much better. But usually, this is a fleeting moment of insight followed by an attack from our ego.

Too often we slip down the rabbit hole of guilt, shame, and self-loathing. Because of the pain this causes, we remove ourselves from that hot seat. We become a victim, and tell the story, "I'm suffering because of what someone else did to me." To solidify it, we gossip. Our story pays us dividends as we receive sympathy from others. All the while, it spreads negativity and causes more pain.

The casualty of becoming a victim in life is that certain important things fall by the wayside; our power, our integrity, quality relationships, Truth, and our connection to Source. It costs a lot to live as a victim. Playing victim for any reason just strengthens the problem. It creates enemies and delays healing. There is another way.

No one wants to fail. We all want positive experiences. We just don't know how to keep bringing them about in our lives. We don't have a formula for when things go wrong. The Ripple Effect Game offers a fantastic way to look at our issues while accepting ourselves—the good, the bad, and the ugly—without falling prey to the ego's defense mechanisms. Instead, we can openly congratulate and lift our personal failures into the light of what they truly are: our biggest avenues for personal awareness, growth, and a wonderful breakthrough. Without harming anyone or feeling guilty at all, we gracefully walk towards the place of insight, every time.

Another problem with not facing our issues is it causes addiction. In order not to feel, we use drugs, alcohol, food, and other types of addictive behavior. When negative things happen, we want a quick-fix for our pain to go away. The Ripple Effect Game is a much healthier solution. The game offers a solution for transmuting this debilitating cycle forevermore.

Speech is powerful. A verbal blow is enough to shut someone down. If someone tells me a particular dress doesn't look good on me, I'll probably never wear it again. We must realize the power of our word, imagine the impact of what we're about to say, and then speak in a way that achieves grace.

I used to believe that the truth always heals. I liked the saying, "We are as sick as our secrets." But now, I realize that there is Divine right timing for messages to be heard. I can be discerning. I believe that being kind is even more honest than speaking out however you feel. People have their own innate council. Most of the time, they don't want our advice, they want to be listened to, and understood. Or just given a hug.

During the game, inviting inquiry into our issues and collecting "points" for each insight makes the process exciting. Reading about someone's breakthrough insights after knowing they were going through a hard week, gives everyone joy.

By the way, who says we shouldn't make mistakes? On the average, an airplane flies off course ~98% of the time. When a commercial airline is on autopilot, it's internal navigation device's system senses thousands of pieces of new data each minute, and simply redirects it's course over and over again, to land safely within inches of it's target. We are just like an airplane on autopilot. Yet we seem to be embarrassed to admit that we're off course.

So, we speak up only after we've already hit something—a car, a sickness, a broken marriage. Why have we defined "admitting we need thousands of corrections" as bad? This is the real question. We need not apologize for being human. We need only to manage being off course.

There is never a reason not to maintain a positive regard for ourselves. Acknowledging and rewarding ourselves through each lesson learned not only ends the cruelty, but can soften the continued bad thoughts. Thus, self-reflection may not be pain free, but it shortens the suffering time. If there's no inquiry, you could be doomed to clobbering yourself indefinitely for an offense of years ago. The ego knows no fairness.

The ability to embrace yourself through difficult change in a way that's full of appreciation will be one of the biggest keys unlocking your full potential. Not allowing any criticism to pollute your self-identity, you can be a bigger loving presence.

This game looks fearlessly in the face of our self-sabotaging ego complex, and melts it. Through the practice of radical non-judgment, and looking for insight in our problems, we free ourselves from denial, addiction, perfectionism, and the blame game. And we get a breakthrough, every time.

Extracting The Positives From the Negatives
(This is where you'll see your own stories!)

Here's my own examples of how I took a negative situation, and turned it around. Imagine this happening to you:

The breakdown:
After a glorious week-long vacation in Cozumel, and after taking hundreds of photos, on the last day, someone stole my iPhone. Confusion swiftly moved to dread as I realized my iPhone was gone. I felt the sickening rush of panic flood my body. I was about to flip out.

This could have collapsed me into a horribly dark mood. I could have obsessed about my loss, ruining the experience of a great vacation. I could have tortured myself, over and over again, for leaving it unattended on my lounge chair. Thankfully, I remembered the breakdown / insights exercise and went to work on it. I came up with the following from the negative situation.

The Insights
- I can replace an iPhone for only $200.

- I could have dropped it in the ocean; at least *someone* is benefitting from it now!
- They must've needed it more than me. Maybe they sold it to buy food, or the necessities of life.
- Most everything in that phone was backed up in my computer.
- I lost some photos, but my new friends from the trip will forward me theirs.

I found five insights. This made me feel quite a bit better. Just for kicks, I decided to keep going and came up with five more:

- I am imagining God is testing me to see how attached I am to material objects. I will win this "test."
- I am recently separated, and I don't need to bring back some of those shots hugging flirty guys, anyway.
- My old iPhone didn't have video capabilities, only a camera. Now I can get one with a video!
- My old camera didn't have as high of a resolution as the new iPhone 4 does. Plus, the new iPhone 4 has so many other perks. Yippee, I'm gonna get an iPhone 4!

And my last positive;
- I get to enjoy the last day of vacation fully available to people, the sights, and the moment, not buried in a mechanical device.

I felt fantastic. I came up with one last one to boot:
- This situation will give me a break for a few days from the heavy electro-magnetic frequencies that smart phones emit. Aaaaaaahh.

My Ripple Effect Journal entry:

"Wow. Not only did I come up with 11 reasons to counteract my devastation, I brainstormed my way into a place of excitement and joy. I feel lighter, more relaxed, and definitely more present. My head was spinning and now it has tingly energy in it. I'm smiling, even laughing a bit, feeling loving compassion for my thief. Now I'm feeling freedom and power. I'm inspired to write. I feel centered, like there's nothing pushing or pulling at me. I'm in my heart, and breathing much easier. I'm returning to thinking about all the great experiences I had on my vacation. I'm so happy. I am one with life~!!"

Here's another real life example.

The Breakdown:
I was at my Mom's house helping her load songs into her iPod, and I lost her whole audio library.

I felt horrible. I couldn't believe it! All those hours of careful work. How could I?!! Well, I couldn't possibly imagine finding any positives, but I knew I had to get myself out of this sad, guilty place. I knew that whatever ideas I might think up could help me. But I couldn't imagine that I'd get anywhere. I proceeded anyway.

The Insights:
- I need to look before I leap. I'm impetuous. This is a recurring pattern.
- Becoming more careful and cautious would better my life.
- I was unfocused because I was inundated with too much stuff on her desk. There are also too many things in my house. I decided to clear away the clutter when I got home.
- I need to move slower. Rushing causes accidents. I can drop into perfect tempo.
- Why was I even doing that? I have too strong an impulse to help people. I can soften that urge.
- What I did wasn't a catastrophe, so no need to make it worse than it was.

Great. There was five insights. Could I find five more?

- Before her music was lost, she got a lesson from me in how to move, delete, and group together music.
- She received virtually all of the songs in her library from a friend whom she can simply ask for an upload again.
- Since she now had no more music, I uploaded her my music library. The next day, she told me she LOVED her new music, songs she'd never heard before.

And lastly,
- I got an opportunity to forgive myself with compassion, for screwing up.

Here's my journal entry:

"I feel way better after doing this exercise. Through this issue, I have learned much. I don't feel elated like I did when doing the exercise on my iPhone loss. But when I took the time to do this exercise, it brought me back my peace of mind within 20 minutes. Not only that, this time it clarified a lot of patterns that don't work for me. I'll take these lessons into my life, and be so much better because of it."

There's an amazing result by finding the many positives in a negative situation. So powerful is this piece, if you do nothing but write 5 insights on all negatives you notice, you would experience non-stop transformation.

Obviously, 5 to 10 insights is an arbitrary number to come up with. When you reach a core insight, you'll know it. Because like a house of cards, the negativity will come toppling down. You'll be able to see things differently in a way that only leaves gratitude in your heart. You know when you've done the exercise right because you'll actually thank the situation for how it changed your life.

It is indeed a very satisfying process to master turning your breakdowns into insights as you reveal for yourself one of life's greatest hidden secrets:

Each tragedy is teaming with blessings.

Chapter 5 — Managing Your Game

The Legend of all Possible Actions

Being witness to, or involved in a **spontaneous blessing**. This is that all-of-the-sudden blessing that occurs, and you realize, "Wow! That was just a blessing." It could be noticing an act of kindness, or receiving something nice. The key to a spontaneous blessing is, you didn't do it; you merely noticed it.

Enacting a **blessing** from the Blessings list found in Chapter 3. This is something you do. It can accomplished in any number of ways: showing love, helping another, giving something, filling a need, offering a smile, having a good thought, sending a prayer, being creative, being good to yourself in some way, or accomplishing a goal.

Reading others' blessings, then **acknowledging** their comments online by clicking "**Nice!**" When you come together in a group, this occurs by listening to each other, and giving acknowledgment to another when you are truly inspired by their share.

Sharing a personal **breakdown**. This becomes material for the various insights you will find. The game isn't only about what's sweet. Write about your struggles!

Insight from your breakdown. Here's the cool part: write all your insights from each breakdown that occurs. Try to find 10. These can be very inspiring to others when it's time to share.

Invention. In the game, this is adding a new Theme or Blessing. I can also be creating music, poetry, artwork, or any creation. It's a new thought or different approach.

Playing the **Bonus Game.** This is where everyone enacts the same blessing at the same time, then writes about their experience. Playing along with the book, the group picks this challenge, then enacts it.

Writing a **Miracle Story**. (About 300 words) Share your most amazing story as a result of playing the Ripple Effect Game.

Vote on your favorite Story. We pick a winning story and/or winning player at the end of each game.

Self-Scoring

This is an optional element for those who thrive on challenge and competition. If you choose to, you can encourage yourself by scoring your activity. One example is as follows:

For every blessing you offer, score 2 credits.
For witnessing a spontaneous blessing, score 1 credit.

For every breakdown you notice, write about it. It scores 2 credits.
For each and every insight you have about the issue, score 1 credit.

For example, with my iPhone story, I get 2 credits for the breakdown, and 11 points for my 11 insights. Then I get 1 credit for the spontaneous good feeling. This exercise scored (2+11+1)= 14 credits.

With losing my mom's music, I get 2 credits for the bummer, and 10 credits for all my insights. Then I get another 2 points because my mom loved her new music she would never have enjoyed if this accident didn't happen, and because that ripple effect made me feel great! This exercise scored (2+10+2)= 14 credits.

New insights can bring about even more ripple effects down the line. So can the current of good energy you've given to another. They in turn pay it forward. When more ripples come, simply add them to your journal, counting more credits for them!

Tallying our score makes for tangible rewards. It can make us feel even better. It's a fun way to deal with our issues, and a rewarding way to collect the pearls. Not only do you get credits, this exercise helps you understand some valuable lessons, while shifting a bad mood into an amazing one. My issues were no longer losses because of looking at them in a new way.

American philosopher, William James, said, "The greatest discovery of my generation is that a human being can alter his life by altering his attitude."

When What You're Doing Doesn't Work

If you're playing the Ripple Effect Game and it feels burdensome, difficult, heavy, a sacrifice, or artificial, then it wasn't a blessing. If it wasn't effortless, sweet, warm or peaceful, something went wrong. But then, this is life too. Life doesn't always snap to our wishes, align itself neatly, or come in bite sized portions. Sometimes it doesn't arrive at the appointed time, but rather like a Mac truck hitting us unexpectedly. As the saying goes, "when it rains, it pours". Another one is, "If you want to make God laugh, tell Him your plans".

Here is a soulful poem you may have heard before. Read it again as if for the very first time. This time, hear it in advance for if you ever want to pick up your ball and leave the playing field. Or when you have collapsed from a breakdown (which surely will come this month) and don't know how to manage. Perhaps "The Invitation" will help you dig deep past the blocks to reignite your weary soul:

"The Invitation"

"It doesn't interest me what you do for a living. I want to know what you ache for and if you dare to dream of meeting your heart's longing.

It doesn't interest me how old you are. I want to know if you will risk looking like a fool for love, for your dream, for the adventure of being alive.

It doesn't interest me what planets are squaring your moon. I want to know if you have touched the centre of your own sorrow, if you have been opened by life's betrayals or have become shrivelled and closed from fear of further pain.

I want to know if you can sit with pain, mine or your own, without moving to hide it, or fade it, or fix it.

I want to know if you can be with joy, mine or your own; if you can dance with wildness and let the ecstasy fill you to the tips of your fingers and toes without cautioning us to be careful, be realistic, remember the limitations of being human.

It doesn't interest me if the story you are telling me is true. I want to know if you can disappoint another to be true to yourself. If you can bear the accusation of betrayal and not betray your own soul. If you can be faithless and therefore trustworthy.

I want to know if you can see Beauty even when it is not pretty every day. And if you can source your own life from its presence.

I want to know if you can live with failure, yours and mine, and still stand at the edge of the lake and shout to the silver of the full moon, 'Yes.'

It doesn't interest me to know where you live or how much money you have. I want to know if you can get up after the night of grief and despair, weary and bruised to the bone and do what needs to be done to feed the children.

It doesn't interest me who you know or how you came to be here. I want to know if you will stand in the centre of the fire with me and not shrink back.

It doesn't interest me where or what or with whom you have studied. I want to know what sustains you from the inside when all else falls away.

I want to know if you can be alone with yourself and if you truly like the company you keep in the empty moments."

-Oriah Mountain Dreamer

We must somehow find that inner fortitude to gather ourselves and pick ourselves up when things go awry. When we're thrown down onto the pavement, we need to get back into the ring. So, love someone *when* you're hurt. Give *because* you're down to heal yourself.

The following are a few pitfalls that can happen, and remedies for consideration. Remember, we are all human. What you did came from a place of good intentions. However, there are no guarantees your interactions will produce great results. The following are some ideas. I'm hoping they are of support.

Problem: Perhaps you became too driven to achieve in this game.

Solution: The goal is to create a myriad of wonderful things, but that can only happen when you're relaxed and surrendered. If you are goal-oriented, then you may not be in the moment. You are likely focused in the future. Being outside of the moment is always being outside of one's own heart. Come back to your heart's desire in this moment and take a breath. Practice meditation more often, preferably today. If you notice yourself becoming too goal-oriented, forget about the points, or how anyone else is doing, and just get into generating good vibes.

Problem: Maybe you feel a loss because your blessing wasn't received.

Solution: But, were *you* able to receive it? That's enough. It's more important that there are no strings attached to your giving. Just give. Let go of any expectations of a gratitude pay back. You buy birthday gifts that you truly love, don't you?

Know this: You have deposited a blessing in the world. You've just accumulated good karma for yourself in your own spiritual bank account by doing this, the only bank account that is eternal. Not only will it come back in unexpected ways, it will come back to you multiplied. Jesus says, "Cast your bread upon the waters and it will come back ten-fold."

Problem: Perhaps you're attached to having positive interactions.

Solution: Make the goal to learn about yourself rather than to feel good, and you will always get a win. For, in every situation are messages of self-understanding, which hold the keys to our growth. Feeling good is never certain, nor should it be consistently counted on. The more we're about the business of building our own character, the more satisfied we will feel.

Problem: Maybe you beat yourself up with that little, mean voice that condemns you when you blow it. "Oh, you idiot! I can't believe you did that! Come on!"

Solution: This negative self-talk must be stopped. Commit to not allowing this menacing voice any "air time." That type of message is never helpful. The moment you catch it, replace it immediately with, "You are such a good person! What a great guy you are!" or "What an amazing woman you are!" Find the phrase that most touches you and repeat it until you feel the Love. Self-defeating feelings and bad-mouthing is un-learned in this way.

Problem: Perhaps you're too analytical and thus, not in the moment.

Solution: Life is a series of spontaneous moments we get to be a part of. Ask, "Am I surrendered? Open-hearted? Do I trust? If not, take a deep breath, and come back to your heart. Go back to your primary intention for playing the game. Listen to your heart's direction, its desires.

Problem: Your body feels out of balance.

Solution: Gently touch your heart and mentally bathe yourself in a feeling of Love for 10 seconds. Then, tune in to your body, and notice some imbalance you were previously unaware of. What does it need right now? What does it say? *Listen,* then respond accordingly.

Some of my worst days in my massage career were because my own body was hungry or tired, and I didn't listen. In hindsight, it was screaming out, abused by a cafe latte with no food, or too many hours before I ate my first meal of the day. I made the connection that conflict or stress in my life multiplied when I didn't eat right! Where do *you* multiply stress or conflict in your life by poor nutrition choices?

Go out of your way to keep yourself fed properly. Love your body through your very best choices each day. Then you can give from a full, replenished cup.

Problem: Days have gone by without playing the game. You have very little time because of a taxing and full schedule.

Solution: Chances are you already give plenty in your life. Fashion plenty of blessings for yourself, filling up that cup of yours. Especially, do this if you have difficulty receiving. Enacting more self-blessings each week could be the life changer.

On another note, if you've gone days and days without playing, please review this period of your life. Become clear about whether you are living in an illusion of getting a lot done, but are really rushed and hectic. Is this helpful? Instead of trying to do it all, try trusting that the more balance you have, the better.

Any way that you can support yourself when what you're doing doesn't work, surely is a blessing. Even the slightest thing, like changing your clothes if they don't feel comfortable, is a great and creative blessing. Give yourself permission to mess up, then make new choices to redirect your course.

In many ways, we need to give ourselves a break. Question that tired old voice and stop being so hard on yourself. Just do what it takes to restore your sanity and your balance. You will eventually come back into that happy place again. If all else fails, remember that tomorrow's another day.

Tips And Ideas

• Live your life as you normally would. When you want to create something positive, let it be natural, gentle and softly potent. Let it be easy.

• Move through the game with a wide open and happy heart.

• Between "quantity" and "quality" moments, in this game strive for quality.

• Don't judge yourself. This only blocks your good from flowing, and cuts off your ability to learn and understand yourself.

- Remember to stay as focused on the ways you can learn through issues as much as when giving and sharing blessings. This is where the breakthroughs lie.

- Ask often and listen keenly for Divine right action at every turn. Trust and surrender to the wisdom within to orchestrate a miracle with ease and grace.

- Never force or push what you think is a good deed onto another. Don't just give blindly; find out what's truly needed first before taking action.

- Don't "forget" to play the game. Try not to go more than 2 days without playing.

- Pay attention to see if your ego is sabotaging you while playing this game in any way. Don't allow your ego to inflate from your own good deeds.

- Refrain from evaluating others along the way. Judgmentalism is never helpful or accurate, and is always hurtful in some way.

- Get out and meet people; this is where the "gold" lies!

- Use this game to "go for it" in life! Stretch yourself beyond your current limits.

- It may seem like bragging to keep sharing all you do. It may feel vulnerable to mention something that's usually kept private. The best medicine is to be honest, simply notice what comes up. Regarding embarrassment, we all take a vow not to judge each other, so sharing is within a safe environment.

- Give yourself plenty of validation and positive strokes. Everything nice you do is 100% precious, timeless, boundless, uniquely valuable, and perfect, just the way it is.

- There's a great surprise awaiting you at the end of the month, so don't give up! Don't ever give up.

- Enjoy! Life is a sweet journey.

Chapter 6 — Blessed

It's All a Blessing

Of course, you could say that everything in life is a blessing, and that one thing you do is just as much a blessing as any other—going to work, watching the children, visiting our friends, doing the dishes. That would be true. But for the purpose of playing this game, what counts is when you become deeply appreciative of an ordinary moment. It generates a positive afterglow in you.

If you find yourself pausing to behold a very special moment, then it is. This happening is like the "ladder square" you land on, when playing the children's board game, *Chutes and Ladders*, that instantly forwards your position in life. It's the check in the mail you didn't expect, or the tickle in you, as you decide to pay for the next few cars at the toll booth. It's the sudden lift you get when you've spent a few more moments appreciating something, helping someone, or maybe letting them help *you*.

A blessing is something simple. It will always feel magical in essence. It will come and have happened before you know it. Blessings are fun, light, freeing. They are funny. They'll tickle your heart.

These blessings happen over and over every day, but we don't notice them. We don't linger in the enjoyment of them long enough. We don't keep track.

It is in the act of a blessing that you will know it. You notice a blessing occurred when you find a new approach to the same old problem, or when you release and let go of a perspective that wasn't working. It happens when you accomplish something important to you, or when you observe something spectacular within the ordinary. Yes, it's all a blessing—but only when you notice.

Forgiveness

**"Out beyond ideas of wrongdoing and rightdoing,
there is a field. I'll meet you there." -Rumi**

We are all human. We make mistakes. Sometimes we act really poorly. So this time, let's not do further harm to us by being hard on ourselves. Let's set aside making judgments as much as possible to have some explorations and fun. Just notice when you withdraw or push against the flow of life, or when you're not being so loving. This is just a habit. Become aware of this, give thanks for the awareness, forgive the whole situation, and then become more compassionate again. That's all you have to do. When you're not being loving, take the time to find 10 insights around it.

To completely forgive a situation, say this **4-part forgiveness exercise** out loud:

"I forgive _____ (person or a situation) for _____ (a harmful situation). And I accept their forgiveness. I forgive myself for _____ (the harmful situation). And I accept my own forgiveness around this."

Now, try these statements on any issue you have. Let it sink in and change the matter. Give yourself time to change. And actually, whether you decide to forgive or not, give yourself the respect of accepting yourself completely, just as you are. This is how you love yourself. During the Ripple Effect Game, you can decide to drop bad habits, and play around with new ways to move through life. You can unlearn negative habit patterns such as rushing, waiting, worrying, and reacting to things poorly.

Stay present to this moment. When you tune out or are "up in your head", thinking about matters of the past or the future, you miss the good stuff. Even if it seems like the present moment is boring, every situation in your life offers you something. Now is where the opportunity is, to be part of an unfolding miracle. When you notice yourself being not present, return to being present. No judgments! Just witness this, and lovingly choose presence.

There is no way to lose the game. There are only degrees of winning, which are attained from the quality and quantity of our newfound awareness. Living in this whole process of offering a blessing, understanding yourself through each action, and noticing all the good feelings you create is quite a miracle in itself. We have not learned to move through life in this way before. We haven't actively sought out ways to help ourselves through helping others for four straight weeks before. We're in a profound new territory.

Acceptance

The moment you begin The Ripple Effect Game, you've already won because playing this game is entering into the consciousness where all is accepted. In his book, *The Power Of Now,* Eckardt Tolle inquires, "Why make an enemy out of the present moment?" Being with what is, is always the first step to self-healing. It's one step before transformation.

I visited a church one Sunday morning. They had a big banner with a slogan that read, "No perfect people allowed." What a relief! The sign was funny, but also comforting. We all want to be accepted, but we don't always accept ourselves. Let's create the room for more acceptance for ourselves, and for others.

There is never a situation without there being a possibility to be of help, to be a force for change, or to be an agent of Love. With this insight, you can understand and accept this moment amidst whatever's going on. You are never again pulled (not for very long, at least) into some crazy pattern of wishing life was different, because you know who you are in the matter. Your new role becomes a saving grace. So you live in a place of calm, knowing each next moment unfolds as it should.

In acceptance, you benefit from everything. You are positive. Life is good. You can become grateful. And even when seemingly nothing is happening, you can enjoy the peace. Being with whatever comes up, you taste the pure delight of existence itself. In acceptance, all is well.

Meditation

Meditation is the path, if you wish to grow. It leads to greater states of freedom. In unlimited ways, it can better your life. Before running out the door to create miracles, first become centered and calm in your whole being. Only when we are quiet, can we listen to that still, small voice within. We are equipped with a governing system that, if we just listen, shares the most beneficial wisdom. It speaks the loving Truth to us. But we need to become quiet inside to hear.

There are a vast number of ways to meditate. Mainly, they all aim at stilling the whirling activity of the mind, opening the heart, and allowing the Eternal Presence to take the forefront. Mainstream life, as we know it, is about things rather than essence. It is all about the temporary. Typically, we dwell in the realm of mind through thoughts of the past and the future. Through meditation, we focus on the Eternal Now, which brings us to the deeper reality. It redirects our focus to the space that holds all things, and into the silence from which all sound arises. Meditation gathers all of your being into right here and right now. It is also the skill of remaining silent and centered in this inner spaciousness.

Meditation has far reaching benefits, replenishing, restoring, and renewing us on all levels. Meditation helps us communicate with our Soul. Once this link is rekindled, we have access to Source. We can experience bliss, deep peace, and deep comfort.

Each time you take the time to go within, your light shines very brightly. You become a beacon to be transformed by your very Father/Mother God who will feel you, and the cries of your heart. It is said the act of pausing to commune with the Source of life is the most precious and rare thing you could do. Your loving focus back to your Creator might be as dear as a new born baby's first smile, as golden as the first kiss of a true love, as treasured as all the riches the world has ever known.

There are numerous ways to meditate. Here is one particular form of meditation I created called the **5-Stage Meditation**.

1)   First, you want to **stretch** for at least 5 to 10 minutes slowly, to open the

body's meridians and free up the life force into your body. When you feel sufficiently stretched, find a proper sitting position where your back is straight but with muscles relaxed. Elevate the tailbone with a pillow.

2)   Take the time to become **quiet** and calm. Let the passing dramas of life go. One way to become real quiet is to focus on the sounds around you. To become very present, focus on the sensations within your body. Listening acutely quiets the mind. Tuning in to the energy sensations in one snapshot helps you to feel your energy-body. You should be feeling balanced.

3)   **Breathe** into the heart in a slow sweet way, as if the air smells exquisite. Breathe out radiating gratitude. Then breathe in bliss up the spine, filling the head. Breathe out even more gratitude very slowly. Now just be blissful gratitude.

4)   Imagine that the Divine is already fully aware of you right now; you are just the part of the equation that was in the waiting. So merely by **making acquaintance** with Masters, ancestors, guides, friends, loved ones, clients, pets, and God, you *are* connected. Continue your loving blissful appreciation as you greet them.

5)   **Return to the center of your being** and **wait receptively** for an energy to come to you in reciprocity after the blissful love you've sent out. Request a wave of greater consciousness. Be in surrendered serenity. Pay attention. Keep returning to this silent moment, releasing ego thoughts, ideas, agendas and stories. Be grateful, realizing something special is happening. Give thanks.
Try this meditation now.

This is how one can harness life force, and attain peak levels of consciousness. It's how you can directly get to peace, balance, joy, gratitude and love, whenever and wherever you want, no matter what your life situation.

Here is another meditation exercise:

Pause a while. Then, recall your greatest joys...your most brilliant accomplishments. Take time to feel this. Now, recall the memory of the best year of your life...a funny moment...your favorite pet...a best friend. Breathe into the feelings of these. Imagine it as a ball of scintillating white-golden light, within your heart. Now imagine this light growing bigger and brighter, feeling more and more wonderful. Whatever positive feeling you have, double it! Breathe this in.

Sit in your feelings, basking in gratitude. Relax. Feel the bliss, the joy, the satisfaction. Settle into a centered place of meditation becoming still for 15 minutes or until you're complete. If thoughts drift, bring them back to the sensation of your slow breath, and the warmth in your heart.

If this way is preferable, meditate this way. In time, you can lengthen your meditation to half an hour, once, then twice per day. This time is never in vain. It energizes your whole being and washes away the stresses in life. Going within can be the most profound of all experiences.

Higher Forces

You don't have to be religious or spiritual to play. The nice thing about it is you needn't believe in anything outside yourself, in order to utilize The Ripple Effect Game for your benefit. Life itself and this book is your complete "kit". Please give yourself full permission to discard any ideas that don't work for you, and just take in the ones that speak to your heart.

Have you ever had an experience of divine orchestration? This is when the many facets of an event come together in perfect timing and flow effortlessly. When we're present, we are actually aligned with a magnificent Universal Energy Field. As we do this, we allow our life to be led and supported by it. It is like a surfer catching a wave. It carries *you* forward, not the other way around. As we let go of controlling how to get our own way, we open up to a whole greater method to bring us what we really want.

We can tap in to the same magnificent Source that governs the stars, that grows all life, that beats our very heart. You will learn to shift from pushing to allowing, from needing to having, from making or willing things to happen, to witnessing spontaneous miracles unfolding every day, as you stay present and receptive to the greater forces at work. How nice it is to know that we aren't in charge of holding up the planet! All we have to do is pay attention to the flow and harmony of the unfolding Plan of life, and follow our hearts.

If you are religious, spend plenty of time communing with God during this month. Actively pray and meditate more than ever. Talk to your Creator about what you truly want in your life. Let it be a prayerful and precious connection you share.

We are guided. We are connected. And we are carried through all our experiences by an unknown force we call by different names. Our daily struggles can cloud the greater actual good we're all a part of. But we can step back a moment and call forth this Grace of God (or Source, Divine, Energy, or Self) to heal anything. Envision waves of Light cascading down upon your situation like a clean surging waterfall. There are a number of ways you can visualize to bring in the greater energies, and unwind the knots in your life. There are unlimited ways to pray.

Rest in the knowledge that your every blessing, like a droplet, sends out a multitude of ripples into the ocean of life. As you give from a place of non-attachment, you will be practicing unconditional Love. When you aren't requiring anything in return, you will feel the freedom and simplicity and sweetness of giving, just for the joy of it.

Your gift of love will be pure, real, and complete. Ironically, letting go of any need for reciprocity will, in turn, make you magnetic to the returns from the world at large. The good will flow abundantly to, and around you. Heaven knows you deserve some good to flow in! Right? Give thanks for it right now.

It is also said, whether we know it or not, that we are all surrounded each and every moment by benevolent Guides whose mission is to help us. We can call on them at any time. They love us dearly, and thrive on being here for us as our guardian angels. They are dedicated to serving, protecting, mentoring, and walking the journey with us, in Love.

Invite your Guides to play The Ripple Effect Game with you! Call upon Spirit to coordinate the most optimum situations for your and everyone's Highest Good. As you continue to align with Higher Guidance, you will feel the blissful Peace that comes when you link up with this field of consciousness. It's OK if you don't feel anything at all. It's enough to keep calling in this support, the protection, special assistance, healing, and Love.

Love

"Teach only love, for that is what you are." —*A Course In Miracles*

If each of the qualities listed in the previous chapters are like keys that will open specific doors on the pathway leading to a promising life, then Love would be the greatest key of all, opening the greatest door.

In the next several weeks, you will learn to generate blessings. This is none other than cultivating the power of Love in your life. Everyone who comes in contact with you will experience this sweet energy you put out, to some degree or another, and will be affected by it. Love is very contagious. Without knowing anything more, you will know you're benefiting others in ways that are priceless and immeasurable.

What a soothing delight to feel when love is unconditional and will always be there. No resentment, no fear, no threats, no anger, and no punishment. True greatness is unselfish love. To forgive someone is to love someone.

It's a nice thing to want love in our lives, but an altogether phenomenal experience to master "Being Love" in all our interactions. The Ripple Effect Game is accomplished through the loving nature within us all. Life is full of opportunities for learning to love. Practice makes perfect. And cultivating blessings is our practice.

If you have known transformation and it did not include love as part of the experience, then all your growth and positive changes are only part fulfilled. They are but a good step in the right direction. Knowing love, exuding this love, and staying in this "Love-Consciousness" is securing the golden key.

Now you have the most important ingredient of the recipe for transformation. It is no secret that love has and always will be the biggest prize in our lives. You have always had this "key to the Kingdom". The Ripple Effect Game merely creates a playground and formula for you to master Love in action.

This is your life, and you are hereby challenged to fulfill its greatest gift. There is nothing more sacred, nothing more important for you to do in your life, than to let your heart be filled with love. If you have loved, you have fulfilled all of life's treasures and have lived a full and complete life. Isn't this the end game we all want?

I will leave you with the paraphrased words of the inspiring 19th century author, Henry Drummond, who illuminates the qualities of love in his book, "The greatest Thing in the World".

"... keep in the midst of life. Be among troubles and difficulties and obstacles. Character grows in the stream of the world's life. Give pleasure. Lose no chance of giving pleasure. For that is the ceaseless and anonymous triumph of a truly loving spirit. He that would be happy, let him remember that there is but one way—it is more blessed to give than to receive.

[Love is] the self-restraint which refuses to make capital out of other's faults; the charity which delights not in exposing the weakness of others, but "covereth all things"; [and is] the sincerity of purpose which endeavors to see things as they are, and rejoices to find them better than suspicion feared or calumny denounced.

What makes a man a good man? Practice. Nothing else. If a man does not exercise his arm he develops no biceps muscle; if a man does not exercise his soul, he acquires no muscle in his soul—no strength of character, no vigor of moral fibre, nor beauty of spiritual growth. Love is not a thing of enthusiastic emotion. And the constitutes of this great character are only to be built up by ceaseless practice."

Final Note

The Ripple Effect Game is a monthly game, but the skills you master will stay with you for life. As you keep offering up all your creative energy again and again, you'll develop habits which return back to you a fortune of good.

Can you imagine what your life would look like if you continued playing the game for a year? What would life on Earth look like if 100 people in many cities across the globe played the Ripple Effect Game, spreading ripples and transmuting injury into insight, for just one month? This is my vision. The game's possibilities are vast and endless.

I look forward to hearing everyone's adventures as the comments and miracle stories pour forth. Feel free to email me at: cindy@rippleeffectgame.com to contribute your innovative ideas to improve this game. In this way, our purpose is lifted to even greater heights for everyone. The Ripple Effect Game belongs to all of us. So please treasure it, and it will become a our treasure.

I bless your journey and your whole life. May this game reveal your shining diamond within, and yield for you all the treasures of your heart. May you take The Ripple Effect Game to new heights, riding a sweet current of miraculous good. Thank you for playing The Ripple Effect Game for Personal and Planetary Transformation. We all benefit from your uniquely magnificent presence in the world.

-Cindy White

Let the game begin!

My

Ripple Effect Game

Journal

PART 2 — MY 30-DAY JOURNAL

My Ripple Effect Game
Journal

Day #1 _____

Today's Theme: _____

Narrative: _____

_____

_____

_____

_____

_____

_____

_____

_____

_____

_____

_____.

My Blessings: _____

_____

_____

_____

_____

_____

_____

_____.

Breakdowns: _____

_____

_____.

Insights: _____

_____

_____

_____.

Day # 2 _____

Today's Theme: _____

Narrative: _____

_____

_____

_____

_____

_____

_____

_____

_____

_____

_____

_____ .

My Blessings: _____

_____

_____

_____

_____

_____

_____

_____

_____.

Breakdowns: _____

_____

_____

_____.

Insights: _____

_____

_____

_____

_____.

Day #3 _____

Today's Theme: _____

Narrative: _____

_____

_____

_____

_____

_____

_____

_____

_____

_____

_____

_____

_____.

My Blessings: _____

_____

_____

_____

_____

_____

_____

_____

_____.

Breakdowns: _____

_____

_____.

Insights: _____

_____

_____

_____.

Day #4 _____

Today's Theme: _____

Narrative: _____

_____

_____

_____

_____

_____

_____

_____

_____

_____

_____

_____

_____ .

My Blessings: _____

_____

_____

_____

_____

_____

_____

_____

_____.

Breakdowns: _____

_____

_____

_____.

Insights: _____

_____

_____

_____

_____.

Day #5 _____

Today's Theme: _____

Narrative: _____

_____

_____

_____

_____

_____

_____

_____

_____

_____

_____

_____

_____ .

My Blessings: _____

_____

_____

_____

_____

_____

_____

_____

_____.

Breakdowns: _____

_____

_____

_____.

Insights: _____

_____

_____

_____

_____.

Day #6 _____

Today's Theme: _____

Narrative: _____

_____

_____

_____

_____

_____

_____

_____

_____

_____

_____

_____

_____ .

My Blessings: _____

_____

_____

_____

_____

_____

_____

_____

_____.

Breakdowns: _____

_____

_____

_____.

Insights: _____

_____

_____

_____.

Day #7 _____

Today's Theme: _____

Narrative: _____

_____

_____

_____

_____

_____

_____

_____

_____

_____

_____

_____

_____.

My Blessings: _____

_____

_____

_____

_____

_____

_____

_____

_____.

Breakdowns: _____

_____

_____.

Insights: _____

_____

_____

_____.

Day #8 _____

Today's Theme: _____

Narrative: _____

_____

_____

_____

_____

_____

_____

_____

_____

_____

_____

_____

_____ .

My Blessings: _____

_____

_____

_____

_____

_____

_____

_____

_____.

Breakdowns: _____

_____

_____.

Insights: _____

_____

_____

_____.

Day #9 _____

Today's Theme: _____

Narrative: _____

_____

_____

_____

_____

_____

_____

_____

_____

_____

_____

_____

_____.

My Blessings: _____

_____

_____

_____

_____

_____

_____

_____

_____.

Breakdowns: _____

_____

_____.

Insights: _____

_____

_____

_____.

Day #10 _____

Today's Theme: _____

Narrative: _____

_____

_____

_____

_____

_____

_____

_____

_____

_____

_____

_____

_____.

My Blessings: _____

_____

_____

_____

_____

_____

_____

_____

_____.

Breakdowns: _____

_____

_____.

Insights: _____

_____

_____

_____.

Day #11 _____

Today's Theme: _____

Narrative: _____

_____

_____

_____

_____

_____

_____

_____

_____

_____

_____

_____.

My Blessings: _____

_____

_____

_____

_____

_____

_____

_____.

Breakdowns: _____

_____

_____

_____.

Insights: _____

_____

_____

_____.

Day #12 _____

Today's Theme: _____

Narrative: _____

_____

_____

_____

_____

_____

_____

_____

_____

_____

_____

_____

_____.

My Blessings: _____

_____

_____

_____

_____

_____

_____

_____

_____.

Breakdowns: _____

_____

_____

_____.

Insights: _____

_____

_____

_____

_____.

Day #13 _____

Today's Theme: _____

Narrative: _____

_____

_____

_____

_____

_____

_____

_____

_____

_____

_____

_____

_____ .

My Blessings: _____

_____

_____

_____

_____

_____

_____

_____

_____.

Breakdowns: _____

_____

_____

_____.

Insights: _____

_____

_____

_____.

Day #14 _____

Today's Theme: _____

Narrative: _____

_____

_____

_____

_____

_____

_____

_____

_____

_____

_____

_____

_____.

My Blessings: _____

_____

_____

_____

_____

_____

_____

_____

_____.

Breakdowns: _____

_____

_____.

Insights: _____

_____

_____

_____

_____.

Day #15 _____

Today's Theme: _____

Narrative: _____

_____

_____

_____

_____

_____

_____

_____

_____

_____

_____

_____

_____ .

My Blessings: _____

_____

_____

_____

_____

_____

_____

_____

_____.

Breakdowns: _____

_____

_____

_____.

Insights: _____

_____

_____

_____

_____.

Day # 16 _____

Today's Theme: _____

Narrative: _____

_____

_____

_____

_____

_____

_____

_____

_____

_____

_____

_____

_____.

My Blessings: _____

_____

_____

_____

_____

_____

_____

_____

_____ .

Breakdowns: _____

_____

_____

_____ .

Insights: _____

_____

_____

_____

_____ .

Day #17 _____

Today's Theme: _____

Narrative: _____

_____

_____

_____

_____

_____

_____

_____

_____

_____

_____

_____

_____.

My Blessings: _____

_____

_____

_____

_____

_____

_____

_____

_____.

Breakdowns: _____

_____

_____.

Insights: _____

_____

_____

_____.

Day #18 _____

Today's Theme: _____

Narrative: _____

_____

_____

_____

_____

_____

_____

_____

_____

_____

_____

_____

_____.

My Blessings: _____

_____

_____

_____

_____

_____

_____

_____

_____.

Breakdowns: _____

_____

_____.

Insights: _____

_____

_____

_____.

Day #19 _____

Today's Theme: _____

Narrative: _____

_____

_____

_____

_____

_____

_____

_____

_____

_____

_____

_____

_____.

My Blessings: _____

_____

_____

_____

_____

_____

_____

_____

_____.

Breakdowns: _____

_____

_____

_____.

Insights: _____

_____

_____

_____

_____.

Day #20 _____

Today's Theme: _____

Narrative: _____

_____

_____

_____

_____

_____

_____

_____

_____

_____

_____

_____

_____.

My Blessings: _____

_____

_____

_____

_____

_____

_____

_____

_____.

Breakdowns: _____

_____

_____

_____.

Insights: _____

_____

_____

_____

_____.

Day #21 _____

Today's Theme: _____

Narrative: _____

_____

_____

_____

_____

_____

_____

_____

_____

_____

_____

_____

_____.

My Blessings: _____

_____

_____

_____

_____

_____

_____

_____

_____.

Breakdowns: _____

_____

_____.

Insights: _____

_____

_____

_____

_____.

Day # 22 _____

Today's Theme: _____

Narrative: _____

_____

_____

_____

_____

_____

_____

_____

_____

_____

_____

_____.

My Blessings: _____

_____

_____

_____

_____

_____

_____

_____

_____.

Breakdowns: _____

_____

_____.

Insights: _____

_____

_____

_____.

Day #23 _____

Today's Theme: _____

Narrative: _____

_____

_____

_____

_____

_____

_____

_____

_____

_____

_____

_____

_____ .

My Blessings: _____

_____

_____

_____

_____

_____

_____

_____

_____.

Breakdowns: _____

_____

_____.

Insights: _____

_____

_____

_____.

Day #24 _____

Today's Theme: _____

Narrative: _____

_____

_____

_____

_____

_____

_____

_____

_____

_____

_____

_____

_____.

My Blessings: _____

_____

_____

_____

_____

_____

_____

_____

_____.

Breakdowns: _____

_____

_____.

Insights: _____

_____

_____

_____

_____.

Day #25 _____

Today's Theme: _____

Narrative: _____

_____

_____

_____

_____

_____

_____

_____

_____

_____

_____

_____

_____.

My Blessings: _____

_____

_____

_____

_____

_____

_____

_____

_____.

Breakdowns: _____

_____

_____

_____.

Insights: _____

_____

_____

_____.

Day #26 _____

Today's Theme: _____

Narrative: _____

_____

_____

_____

_____

_____

_____

_____

_____

_____

_____

_____

_____.

My Blessings: _____

_____

_____

_____

_____

_____

_____

_____

_____.

Breakdowns: _____

_____

_____

_____.

Insights: _____

_____

_____

_____

_____.

Day #27 _____

Today's Theme: _____

Narrative: _____

_____

_____

_____

_____

_____

_____

_____

_____

_____

_____

_____

_____.

My Blessings: _____

_____

_____

_____

_____

_____

_____

_____

_____.

Breakdowns: _____

_____

_____.

Insights: _____

_____

_____

_____.

Day #28 _____

Today's Theme: _____

Narrative: _____

_____

_____

_____

_____

_____

_____

_____

_____

_____

_____

_____

_____

_____.

My Blessings: _____

_____

_____

_____

_____

_____

_____

_____

_____.

Breakdowns: _____

_____

_____.

Insights: _____

_____

_____

_____.

Day #29 _____

Today's Theme: _____

Narrative: _____

_____

_____

_____

_____

_____

_____

_____

_____

_____

_____

_____

_____

_____.

My Blessings: _____

_____

_____

_____

_____

_____

_____

_____

_____.

Breakdowns: _____

_____

_____

_____.

Insights: _____

_____

_____

_____

_____.

Day #30 _____

Today's Theme: _____

Narrative: _____

_____

_____

_____

_____

_____

_____

_____

_____

_____

_____

_____.

My Blessings: _____

_____

_____

_____

_____

_____

_____

_____.

Breakdowns: _____

_____

_____.

Insights: _____

_____

_____

_____

Game finished!   Congratulations!!!!!!!!!

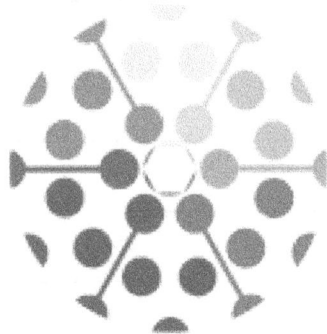

~My Miracle Stories~

Please write your miracle stories in the following pages.
Then, post them on the site, www.RippleEffectGame.com
Thank you!!

Always know that YOU are the blessing

PART 3 — MY STORIES

Miracle Story

_____

_____

_____

_____

_____

_____

_____

_____

_____

_____

_____

_____

_____

_____

_____

_____

_____

_____

Miracle Story

_____

_____

_____

_____

_____

_____

_____

_____

_____

_____

_____

_____

_____

_____

_____

_____

_____

_____

_____

Miracle Story

_____

_____

_____

_____

_____

_____

_____

_____

_____

_____

_____

_____

_____

_____

_____

_____

_____

_____

_____

Miracle Story

_____

_____

_____

_____

_____

_____

_____

_____

_____

_____

_____

_____

_____

_____

_____

_____

_____

_____

_____

The most wonderful moments I experienced this month:

_____

_____

_____

_____

_____

_____

_____

_____

_____

_____

My biggest breakdowns and their insights this month:

_____

_____

_____

_____

_____

_____

_____

_____

_____

_____

_____

_____.

_____

_____

_____

Some profound personal changes I incorporated this month:

_____

_____

_____

_____

_____

_____

_____

_____

_____

_____

_____

_____.

Glossary of Terms and Definitions

Blessing: An offering or act of Love, either deliberate (as in to bless the meal) or randomly occurring (when it stops raining before a wedding). There is always a witness or someone involved who is sweetly moved.

Breakdown: The unexpected negative outcome of an action or event, usually involving hard feelings, struggle, and disappointment. Broken. Stopped.

Game: A formula with strategy and rules agreed to by all, having the goal of learning, mastering talents, winning, and/or having fun. Creative play.

Insight: A new perspective which reveals deeper meanings than an obvious, superficial one, a clue which releases a breakdown. An aha!

Lesson: Having integrated a variety of meanings from a past activity (as in a lesson learned), or understanding a topic (as in a golf lesson)

Meditation: An enhanced awareness and clear, deep presence attained by consciously stilling the mind. It is usually practiced by sitting for periods, but is also achieved by many methods; chanting, a walk through nature, sports activities, gazing on a candle flame. Meditation can be solo or in a group.

Miracle: A massive convergence of good (as in a miracle come true), doing the seemingly impossible (a miraculous feat), beholding anything with great awe, (like when star gazing), a fantastic, beautful mystery (the miracle of life).

Ripple effect: Concentric waves or vibrations which emanate outward and inward infinitely, caused by one simple action—such as a pebble cast into a pool of water. A domino effect. The cumulative effect of this domino effect.

Theme: A constant and/or recurring mode of being (as in theme of the day). The main plot (as in a story).

Transformation: A radical shift of consciousness into a pure, clear, loving, or otherwise deeply enhanced way.

The Meaning of Our Logo

Take another look at the cover of this book. The Ripple Effect Game's symbol is a multi-colored circular image of little balls, half balls, and rods. This was specifically designed for many reasons. In an ancient language, the symbol is called "Ta Tou." The Ta Tou is defined as a cosmic force that organizes chaos into unity and beauty.

Commonly known as the "dandelion symbol" Ta Tou directs random forces, converging and synchronizing them, to create an expression of beauty and flow, as does the game. In nature the dandelion is a weed we pick, and make a wish to, as we blow off its seeds. And as the wives tale goes, if we blow them all off, our wish comes true. When you play the Ripple Effect Game, your "dream life" comes true!

If the ball is the Earth, the rods emanate out as if to reach to the ends of the Earth to bless all of mankind everywhere. Multicolored, it represents the total diversity of all humankind and life, together making one multi-faceted organized whole.

Our symbol is a key for shifting into a new paradigm of thinking and acting, creating universal wholeness and loving inter-connectedness throughout the Web of Life. From the quantum vacuum, to atoms and our DNA, to galaxies, there are reoccuring ratios and geometric symmetries at the foundation of the whole cosmos.

Our geometric shape is the hexagram. It is "sacred geometry" meaning the building blocks of life itself. The hexagram shows up in myth and in many religions. It is the anahata, or heart chakra. The hexagram is the Flower of Life. An intersection of two triangles, it is the star of David, a symbol of many interpretations, but one definition is that of union between man and God, and the "as above, so below" principle.

On a more whimsical note, the ball looks like that suction-cupped sticky toy you throw to make stick on the wall. Just like the Ripple Effect Game, it's simply a fun game to play!

For all of these reasons, the symbol Ta Tou is the perfect represention for our game.

Bibliography and Reading List

The Holy Bible

Loving What Is, Byron Katie

The Four Agreements, Don Miguel Ruiz

A Course In Miracles, Dr. Helen Schucman and William Thetford

Science Of Mind, Ernest Holmes

The Power Of Now, and *A New Earth*, Eckhardt Tolle

The Law Of Attraction, Abraham-Hicks

"I Have A Dream...", a speech by Dr. Martin Luther King, Jr.

A Simple Path, Mother Theresa

The Door Of Everything, Ruby Nelson

Autobiography of A Yogi, Paramahansa Yogananda

Zuan Falun, Master Li Honzhi

Hands Of Light, Barbara Ann Brennan

Be Here Now, Ram Dass

The Dark Side Of The Light Chasers, Debbie Ford

Conversations With God, An Uncommon Dialogue, Neal Donald Walsch

Illusions, Adventures Of a Reluctant Messiah, Richard Bach

The Road Less Traveled, M. Scott Peck

References

The World Wide Web

Dictionary.com

Centers for Disease Control and Prevention

Accessing Inner Guidance, the 5-D teachings, and the Ta Tou', Dr. Valerie Girard

SchoolOfSacredGeometry.com

The Gohanzon and Nam Myoho Renge Kyo, Nishirin Dishonin Buddhism

The practice of Yoga

The practice of Meditation

About the Author

Cindy M. White is a lifelong healer and business woman living in Santa Barbara, CA. She is a Massage Therapist, Speaker, Designer, and Author.

Graduating from The Institute For Educational Therapy in Berkeley, California in 1989, Cindy obtained her license in Massage Therapy and Movement Therapy. She received her Clinical Hypnotherapist Certification from Heartwood Institute in 1992.

In private practice for 24 years, she teaches classes, workshops, retreats, and college programs in health and wellness. For more information visit: www.CindyWhite.org.

White's publications include: *You Get There By Being There, a Symphony of Spiritual Quotes*, and *101 Answers For My Beloved, the Necessary Questions to Create Happily Ever After*. To come are: *Crazy Useless Concepts and getting free of them*, and *The Awareness Eating Plan*.

Cindy enjoys a variety of activities including meditation, yoga, skiing, diving, golf, dance and travel. With a zest for life and a joyous spirit, Cindy's passion is to inspire greater health and the awakening to the magnificence of our true nature, found within our hearts.

E-mails / Phone numbers / Notes

E-mails / Phone numbers / Notes

_____

_____

_____

_____

_____

_____

_____

_____

_____

_____

_____

_____

_____

_____

_____

_____

_____

_____

E-mails / Phone numbers / Notes

www.ingramcontent.com/pod-product-compliance
Lightning Source LLC
LaVergne TN
LVHW061259060426
835509LV00013B/1495

9 780615 710167